Fact Finders®

SCARY
SCIENCE

MUTANT ANIMALS
CRAZY CREATURES ALTERED BY SCIENCE

BY SALLY LEE

CONSULTANT:
MICHAEL D. BENTLEY, PHD
PROFESSOR, DEPARTMENT OF BIOLOGICAL SCIENCES
MINNESOTA STATE UNIVERSITY, MANKATO

CAPSTONE PRESS
a capstone imprint

Fact Finders Books are published by Capstone Press,
1710 Roe Crest Drive, North Mankato, Minnesota 56003
www.capstonepub.com

Library of Congress Cataloging-in-Publication Data
Lee, Sally.
Mutant animals : crazy creatures altered by science / by Sally Lee.
pages cm.—(Fact finders. scary science)
Includes bibliographical references and index.
Summary: "Describes various animals that have been genetically altered by scientists"—Provided
by publisher.
ISBN 978-1-4765-3929-4 (library binding) — ISBN 978-1-4765-5127-2 (paperback) — ISBN 978-1-4765-5976-6
(ebook pdf)
1. Transgenic animals. 2. Animal genetic engineering. 3. Animal mutation breeding. 4. Animal
genetics. I. Title.
QH442.6.L43 2014
616.02'73—dc23   2013025787

Editorial Credits
Jennifer Besel, editor; Veronica Scott, designer; Marcie Spence, media researcher;
    Eric Manske, production specialist

Photo Credits
AP Images: Mayo Clinic/Rex Features, 15; AquaBounty Technologies Inc., 19; Capstone Studio: Karon Dubke,
4; Corbis: Reuters, 24; Courtesy of Charles Alfred Vacanti, M.D., cover, 8; Getty Images: 27, Edward Kinsman,
17, Graham Crouch, 22, Mary Beth Angelo, 23, Sovfoto, 7; Shutterstock: Csehak Szabolcs, 16, dotweb Steen B
Nielsen, 5, oksana2010, 10, Ragne Kabanova, 28, 29, riekephotos, 21, Steshkin Yevgeniy, 20, talseN, 13, vitstudio:
4–5

Printed in the United States of America in Stevens Point, Wisconsin.
092013   007769WZS14

TABLE OF CONTENTS

CHAPTER 1

MIXED-UP ANIMALS

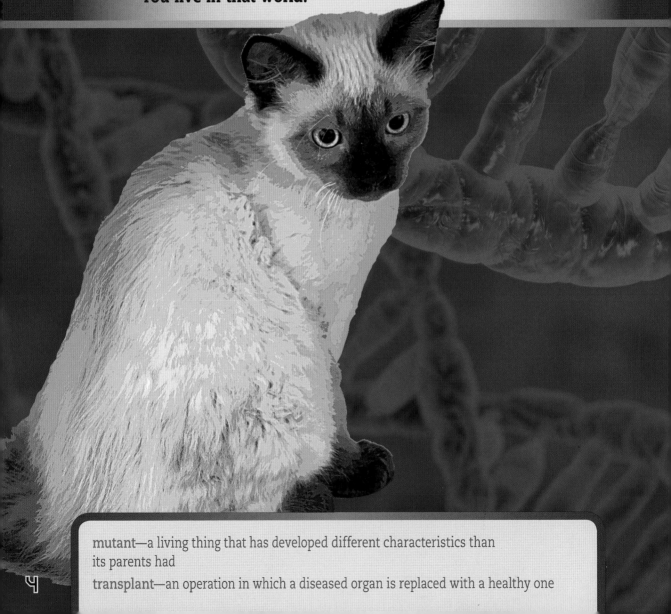

Imagine a world with two-headed dogs. Mice with ears on their backs. Kittens that glow in the dark. You live in that world.

mutant—a living thing that has developed different characteristics than its parents had

transplant—an operation in which a diseased organ is replaced with a healthy one

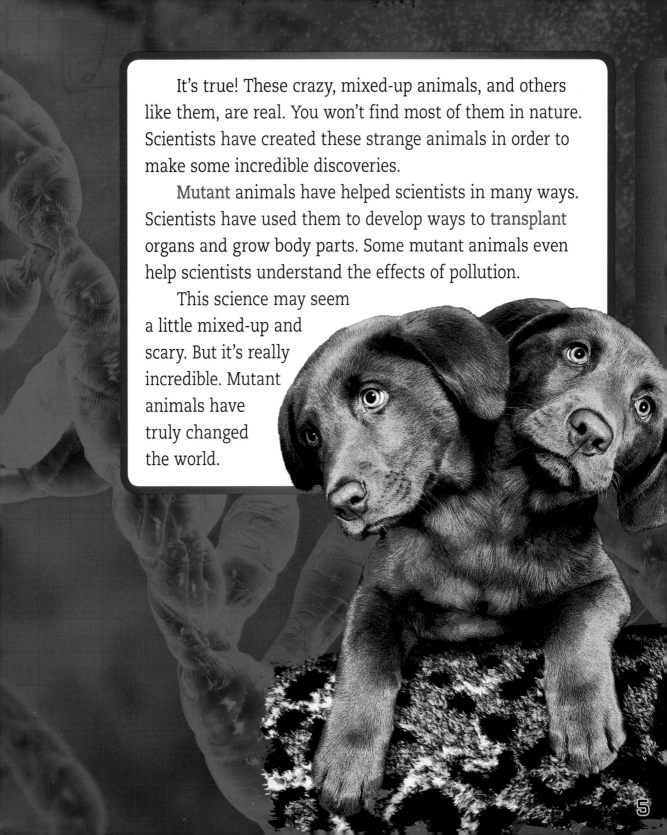

It's true! These crazy, mixed-up animals, and others like them, are real. You won't find most of them in nature. Scientists have created these strange animals in order to make some incredible discoveries.

Mutant animals have helped scientists in many ways. Scientists have used them to develop ways to transplant organs and grow body parts. Some mutant animals even help scientists understand the effects of pollution.

This science may seem a little mixed-up and scary. But it's really incredible. Mutant animals have truly changed the world.

CHAPTER 2

STRANGE-LOOKING EXPERIMENTS

In the 1940s and 1950s Russian scientist Vladimir Demikhov created 20 two-headed dogs. Demikhov surgically attached the head and front legs of a puppy onto an adult dog's neck.

The adult's heart pumped blood to both heads. Even without a body, the puppy was playful. It nipped the dog's ears and licked people's hands. It even drank milk from a bowl. The longest one of these two-headed dogs lived was just one month. But what Demikhov learned from these experiments was priceless.

Demikhov was a heart surgeon trying to find a way to save human lives. He wanted to prove that a body could support new organs. His two-headed dog experiments did just that. Demikhov proved that organ transplants were possible.

Today about 79 people receive organ transplants every day. Without Demikhov's two-headed dogs, those surgeries might have never been possible.

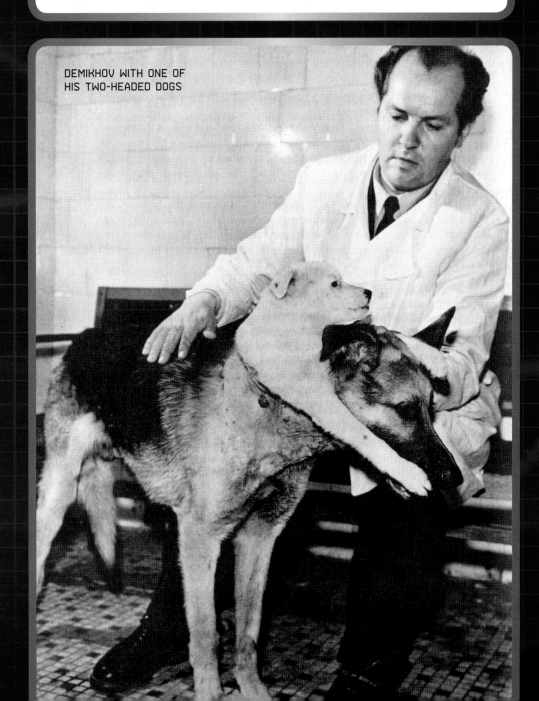

DEMIKHOV WITH ONE OF HIS TWO-HEADED DOGS

EARMOUSE

Ears are easy to damage. A person's outer ear can easily tear in a car or sports accident. But repairing an ear is difficult. Having new ears to transplant onto people would be extremely helpful. That's where the earmouse comes in.

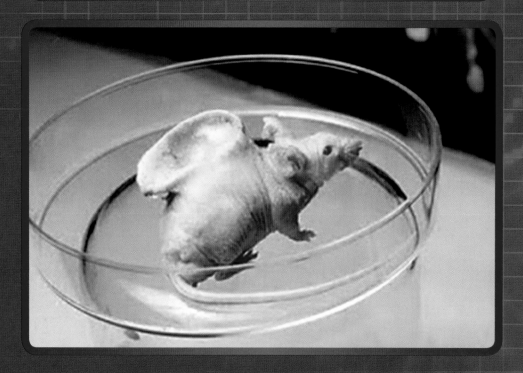

dissolve—to disappear into something else

cartilage—a strong, rubbery tissue that connects bones in people and animal

Dr. Joseph Vacanti created this odd-looking mouse in 1997. He started with a frame in the shape of a human ear. The frame was made of material that would dissolve over time. Then he covered the frame with cow cartilage cells. Once the ear frame was ready, Vacanti placed it under the back skin of a hairless mouse.

The mouse's body kept the new cells supplied with blood while they grew. Over three months the cartilage cells filled in the frame, and the frame dissolved. There, on the back of a mouse, was a structure that looked just like a human ear. The ear could then be removed without hurting the mouse at all.

Thanks to earmouse, scientists know much more about growing simple tissues such as skin and blood vessels. Now scientists can make hollow organs such as stomachs. Someday it may be possible to grow a heart.

FACT:

ONE WOMAN HAD HER OUTER EAR REMOVED BECAUSE OF CANCER. THANKS TO WHAT THEY LEARNED FROM EARMOUSE, DOCTORS WERE ABLE TO GROW A NEW EAR ON THE WOMAN'S ARM. AFTER FOUR MONTHS THEY TOOK IT OFF HER ARM AND PUT IT WHERE IT BELONGED. THIS PROCEDURE IS NOW USED OFTEN.

CHANGING THE CODE

Spider goat. Is it a goat with eight legs or a spider with horns? Neither. These mixed-up animals look just like regular goats. It's their milk that's spectacular. Spider goat milk can be used to make spider silk!

Spider silk is better than any human-made fibers for stitching up wounds or making tough fabrics. But you can't raise spiders to get their silk. When they get crowded, spiders eat each other.

So scientists got creative. They took the silk-making **genes** from spiders and put them into goats. The goats' bodies then started making the same **protein** spiders make. The protein came out in their milk.

SPIDER GOATS LOOK JUST LIKE REGULAR GOATS. ONLY THEIR MILK IS DIFFERENT.

Scientists take proteins from the milk and squeeze them through a tube. The proteins get squished together into a thread. The thread is thinner than a human hair. But it's strong enough to make a bulletproof vest. Now goats make more silk than spiders. And they don't eat each other.

PUTTING THE GENES ON

Every living thing is made up of trillions of cells. Inside each cell, DNA carries all the instructions for life. DNA is made up of sections called genes. The genes tell the cells what traits the person, animal, or plant will have.

Today scientists can give animals traits from other animals. First they find the gene that controls that trait. Then they snip it out and stick it into the DNA of another animal that is just beginning to grow. As the animal grows, its cells divide, creating new cells that all have the new genes. When the baby is born, it has the new trait. This process is called genetic engineering.

gene—a part of every cell that carries physical and behavioral information passed from parents to their children
protein—a chemical made by animal and plant cells to carry out various functions
trait—a quality or characteristic that makes one person or animal different from another

FOUR-LEGGED FACTORIES

Believe it or not, mutant animals are helping make medicines too. Blood clots are a dangerous condition for some people. These clumps of blood clog up veins and arteries, stopping blood from reaching the heart or brain.

Patients take medicine to stop clots from forming. But some people's bodies can't handle the regular medicine. They need a special one made from proteins found in human blood. But it's hard to get enough blood to make the drug. Animals to the rescue! Scientists gave goats the human genes needed to make the protein. Now the protein is in the goat's milk.

FACT:

ONE GOAT CAN PRODUCE MORE THAN 6 POUNDS (3 KILOGRAMS) OF THE CLOT-BLOCKING PROTEINS IN A YEAR. IT WOULD TAKE 90,000 BLOOD DONATIONS TO GET THE SAME AMOUNT FROM HUMANS.

PIG PARTS

Each year thousands of people need organ transplants. But there aren't enough organs available. Many people die before the right one is found. Using organs from pigs could ease this shortage.

It sounds strange, but pigs are more like humans than you think. Some of their organs should work in humans. But there's a problem. A human's immune system doesn't like strange things in its body. It rejects the organs by attacking them. Now scientists are trying to add human genes to some pigs. Having human genes could fool the immune system into accepting the organ. Pig arteries are already used to help patients with heart problems. Someday more people may be alive because of pig parts.

immune system—the part of the body that protects against germs and diseases

ALL AGLOW

What do you get when you mix the genes from a cat, a monkey, and a jellyfish? You get spooky kittens that glow green. But these kittens may help save lives.

AIDS is a disease caused by the HIV virus. AIDS damages a person's immune system. Patients die when their bodies can't fight off other diseases. Cats and monkeys can get viruses similar to HIV.

But one kind of monkey makes a protein that blocks the virus. Scientists wondered if the protein could work in cats too. They put the monkey gene in cats to pass on to their kittens.

But scientists needed a way to tell if the kittens got the monkey gene. So they also gave the mother cats the gene that makes crystal jellyfish glow. If the kittens glowed, scientists would know they had the new genes. The experiment was a success. Cells taken from these glowing kittens blocked the virus. Scientists hope they can use this information to find a way to block HIV in humans.

ENVIROPIG

Scientists use genetic engineering to help the environment too. You see, there's a problem with pig poop. And the problem isn't the smell. Pig poop contains too much of a chemical called phosphorus.

Food has phosphorus in it. Most animals have an **enzyme** in their bodies that helps them **digest** the chemical. But pigs don't have that enzyme. Most of their phosphorus ends up in steaming piles of poo.

WHEN PHOSPHORUS WASHES INTO LAKES AND RIVERS, THE WATER BECOMES OVERGROWN WITH ALGAE.

enzyme—a protein that helps break down food
digest—to break down food so it can be used by the body

Farmers spread pig poop on their fields. But when it rains, that poop washes into rivers and lakes. Algae in the water feast on the phosphorus and grow. When algae grow too large, they use up the oxygen in the water. Without enough oxygen, fish and marine plants die.

To fix the problem, scientists found a gene in bacteria that digests phosphorus. Another gene from mice makes the bacteria's gene copy itself. They put these genes in pigs. The result is Enviropig—a pig with poop that's better for the environment. That definitely doesn't stink.

FISHING FOR CHEMICALS

Factories often dump chemicals into lakes and rivers. Nobody likes swimming with chemicals, especially fish. It makes them sick. But scientists couldn't tell which parts of the fish's bodies were being harmed.

Scientists put a gene from crystal jellyfish into zebra fish eggs. When the babies hatched, scientists exposed them to different chemicals. The fish's bodies glowed wherever the chemicals were doing damage. Scientists could see the glowing through the babies' thin, see-through skin.

MUTANT FOOD

Sometimes genetic engineering is used to change animals that people eat. Scientists are working to make food healthier and more available.

Salmon is a popular and healthy food. But salmon grow pretty slowly. It takes about three years for one to reach full size. So scientists created super salmon. These mutant fish grow two times faster than regular salmon. And they taste exactly the same.

hormone—a chemical made by a gland in the body that affects growth and development

A couple of extra genes make these super salmon grow faster. Scientists used a gene from a Chinook salmon that makes a growth **hormone**. They also used a gene from a long eel-like fish called an ocean pout. The ocean pout's gene keeps the salmon growing during the winter. With these genes super salmon grow all year long. They reach full size in 18 months instead of three years.

A SUPER SALMON AND AN ATLANTIC SALMON OF THE SAME AGE ARE DRASTICALLY DIFFERENT IN SIZE.

BETTER BACON

How about some worms with breakfast? OK, worms probably won't be on many breakfast menus. But someday your bacon may come from pigs that have worm genes.

One kind of earthworm makes omega-3 fatty acids. These acids are fats that are good for your heart and brain. You can find omega-3s in fish, but not in meat. Pigs are full of saturated fat. This kind of fat clogs arteries and causes heart problems.

Scientists gave some pigs a gene from earthworms. The result is pork that has more good fats and fewer bad ones. Someday these piggies might make it to market, and you'll have less fatty bacon to eat.

BREEDING FOR TRAITS

Some mixed-up animals weren't created in labs. When two animals that don't normally mate are bred together, their young are called hybrids. Hybrids get traits from both parents. So they can be a little bit strange.

A cama has a camel for a father and a llama for a mother. It was created to produce more wool and meat than a regular llama.

Male dzo or female dzomo are the offspring of a yak and a common cow. Most of these hybrids live in the mountains of Tibet. Dzos are strong. They can carry heavy loads and plow fields. They also produce more milk and meat than cows.

FARMERS IN INDIA USE DZOS TO HAUL EQUIPMENT.

breed—to mate and raise a certain kind of animal

Beefalo are hybrids of the American buffalo and beef cattle. Like buffalo these animals can live on land too rugged for cattle. Beefalo meat has more protein and less fat than normal beef.

Zebroids are hybrid zebras. One parent is a zebra. The other parent is either a donkey, horse, or pony. Zebroids were originally bred as pack animals in Africa. A zebra and a donkey make a zedonk or zedonkey. A zebra-pony mix is a zony. And a zorse is a zebra and a horse.

A ZORSE GRAZING IN KENYA, AFRICA

NEARLY NAKED

Chickens are supposed to have feathers. So why are some chickens in Israel wearing nothing but red wrinkled skin? Scientists there say the weather is too hot for feathers. The hot chickens don't grow well. To solve the problem, they bred normal broiler chickens with naked-neck chickens. The result is cooler naked chickens that grow faster and are lower in calories.

Raising featherless chickens may make sense for some areas. The chickens can use their energy to grow and not waste it on making feathers. And they are cooler without their feather coats. Also, farmers don't have to spend a lot of money plucking feathers.

Some scientists think the naked chickens are a bad idea, though. They say without feathers, the birds are more likely to be sunburned or bitten by mosquitoes. Only time will tell if the naked chicken idea will take flight.

NOT-SO-WOOLY SHEEP

Farmers have used breeding to make some odd sheep too. Wrestling with a sheep to cut off its wool isn't fun. And when the price of wool is low, it's not worth the effort. Some farmers in England found a good answer. They bred female sheep with rams that shed their wool each year. Now each spring, the hybrid sheep shed their winter coats. In the fall they grow new ones.

MAKING A COPY

Every animal is unique. When scientists breed animals, the young all have similar traits. But they have some differences. It's the same with people. But scientists have found a way to create copies of animals. These animals are exactly the same, inside and out. This procedure is called cloning.

In 1996 scientists cloned the first mammal. They took a cell from an adult sheep and put it in an egg cell. The two cells merged together and began dividing. The cells grew into another sheep exactly the same as the first. Scientists named the sheep Dolly.

In 2008 scientists in Japan used the same technique to clone mice. They created 581 mice that were all exact copies of each other.

This kind of cloning might be useful. It could be used to rebuild populations of endangered animals. However, some experiments show that cloning can cause animals to develop health problems. Also, some people worry that cloning is ethically wrong.

ethic—a belief in doing what is right

DOLLY, THE WORLD'S FIRST
CLONED MAMMAL

HELPFUL MIX-UPS

It's hard to imagine life without mixed-up animals.
They help make medicines. They provide food. They even
help clean up the environment.

Mutant animals aren't done helping out. In the future they'll likely help scientists find cures for more diseases. People who need transplants might even get their organs from them. In a world where goats can make spider silk, anything is possible.

GLOSSARY

breed (BREED)—to mate and raise a certain kind of animal

cartilage (KAHR-tuh-lij)—a strong, rubbery tissue that connects bones in people and animals

digest (dy-GEST)—to break down food so it can be used by the body

dissolve (di-ZOLV)—to disappear into something else

enzyme (EN-zime)—a protein that helps break down food

ethic (ETH-ik)—a belief in doing what is right

gene (JEEN)—a part of every cell that carries physical and behavioral information passed from parents to their children

hormone (HOR-mohn)—a chemical made by a gland in the body that affects growth and development

immune system (i-MYOON SISS-tuhm)—the part of the body that protects against germs and diseases

mutant (MYOOT-uhnt)—a living thing that has developed different characteristics than its parents had

protein (PROH-teen)—a chemical made by animal and plant cells to carry out various functions

trait (TRATE)—a quality or characteristic that makes one person or animal different from another

transplant (TRANSS-plant)—an operation in which a diseased organ is replaced with a healthy one

READ MORE

Barber, Nicola. *Cloning and Genetic Engineering.* Both Sides of the Story. New York: Rosen Publishing's Rosen Central, 2013.

Duke, Shirley Smith. *You Can't Wear These Genes.* Let's Explore Science. Vero Beach, Fla.: Rourke Pub., 2011.

Lee, Sally. *Mad Scientists: The Not-So-Crazy Work of Amazing Scientists.* Scary Science. North Mankato, Minn.: Capstone Press, 2014.

INTERNET SITES

FactHound offers a safe, fun way to find Internet sites related to this book. All of the sites on FactHound have been researched by our staff.

Here's all you do:

Visit *www.facthound.com*

Type in this code: 9781476539294

Check out projects, games and lots more at
www.capstonekids.com

INDEX